D0065127

A New Mother's Thoughts

Poems by Jayne Jaudon Ferrer

Illustrated by Lina Levy

POCKET BOOKS

New York • London • Toronto • Sydney • Tokyo • Singapore

Grateful acknowledgment is made to Zondervan Publishing
for permission to reprint previously published material from
Honey for a Child's Heart by Gladys Hunt.
Copyright © 1978 Gladys Hunt.

POCKET BOOKS, a division of Simon & Schuster Inc.
1230 Avenue of the Americas, New York, NY 10020

Copyright © 1989 by Jayne Jaudon Ferrer

All rights reserved, including the right to reproduce this book or
portions thereof in any form whatsoever. For information, address
Pocket Books, 1230 Avenue of the Americas, New York, NY 10020

ISBN: 0-671-56844-2

First Pocket Books hardcover printing May 1996

10 9 8 7 6 5 4 3 2 1

POCKET and colophon are registered trademarks of
Simon & Schuster Inc.

Book design by Patrice Kaplan and Gina Bonanno

Printed in Mexico

*For John Lawrence,
who still makes
motherhood wonderful.*

Acknowledgments

When I first wrote this book, I was an innocent—a mother inexperienced in events and emotions outside the realm of those first few wonderful years. I still don't know what it's like to lose a child, or have one break your heart, but I do know that seven years and two more children later, I still believe motherhood offers the most exhilarating, exhausting, painful, and precious moments a woman ever knows.

I am grateful to many for their love and support in my often frustrating pursuit of twin passions. Time schedules for writing books and raising a family frequently conflict; I appreciate the willingness of my husband and sons to eat leftovers and let me sleep late on Saturdays. I thank my own mother for always believing in me, my "Aunt" Reta for her gentle wisdom and positive outlook on life, Jim Kelly for putting my first words in print three decades ago, and Mrs. Ertzberger for teaching me how to write a good outline.

𝕵o mothers reading this: cherish your children and remember to record your own special moments.

𝕵o husbands reading this: in a recent unscientific survey, three out of four new mothers said the gift they wanted most was this book and more sleep.

𝕵o others reading this: ditto the above, and a couple of casseroles never hurt, either.

Happy mothering—
J.J.F.

Thoughts for Moments of Gratification

Beat upon mine! little heart! beat, beat!
Beat upon mine! You are mine, my sweet!
All mine from your pretty blue eyes
to your feet, My sweet!
Alfred Lord Tennyson

PRAYER OF GRATITUDE

Father, You gave me an angel.
  Straight from heaven,
born on earth,
this child rests here in my arms,
purity personified,
innocence ensconced
in the essence of perfection.
Mere hours old,
already she has filled our lives
with joy and light and love.
One tiny emissary of peace,
one unblemished hope
for tomorrow's happiness.
Praise to You, Father,
for this most precious gift You've shared.
Pleas to You, Father,
for aid in raising her to be
always
as self-contented as she is today.

THE PLAY'S THE THING

Forgive me, Lord,
for all the tasks
that went undone today.
But this morning when my child
toddled in and said, "Mommy play?,"
I simply had to say yes.
And between the puzzles and trucks
and blocks and dolls and old hats and
books and giggles,
we shared a thousand special thoughts,
a hundred hopes and dreams and hugs.
And tonight, when prayer time came
and he folded his hands and softly whispered,
"Thank you, God, for Mommy and Daddy and
toys and french fries, but 'specially
for Mommy playing,"
I knew it was a day well wasted.
And I knew You'd understand.

JIGSAW

In utter amazement,
I watch her, God.
Like an architect intent on perfection,
she twists and turns each puzzle piece
till—all at once—it plops into place.
They charm her, these tiny multicolored
snippets of Mickey and Minnie.
Interwoven, interlocked…
some edges smooth and simple;
others jagged, erratic, and sharp.
Her life will be as this puzzle, Lord—
confusing, chaotic, and incomplete….
But surely, succinctly, day by day,
she will learn to finagle each fragment
into place,
slowly working her way toward wholeness.

I see signs of it even now—
pensive observation of two friends
fighting over a toy…
scrutinizing questions to confirm her hunch
(and hope) that monsters aren't real…
giddy, unchecked glee in discovering that
she, too, can pull one over on Dad.
Dear God, be with us all
as her life pieces grow into place.
Guide her labyrinthian quest for fulfillment.
Give her wisdom to solve each new quandary,
and help me harness my urge to assist
until she asks.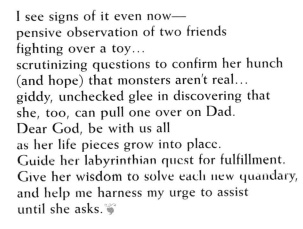

Thoughts for Moments of Exhaustion

❧

But in the midst of her glad wonderment
She found herself besieged and overcome....
Edwin Arlington Robinson

Superwoman's Lament

O kay, God, that's it.
I quit.
Even I—Former Cheerleader,
Clairol-Tressed
RealWomanoftheNinetiesDressedforSuccess,
Mother Superior, and
Coupon Clipper/Refunder Extraordinaire—
can't do it all.
Could You? I wonder.
Even with Egg McMuffins
and Velcro shoes
and grocery delivery
and a reliable sitter,
there's still PMS
and 10-day check holds
and 100-piece Duplo sets
and wet sheets in the middle of the night.
And not even IBM
has come up with a machine to handle

bill-paying, menu-planning,
job-keeping, house-cleaning,
story-reading, eyebrow-tweezing,
shirt-ironing, dog-walking, and
libido-satisfying all at once.
I'd pray for a maid, God, but
I can't afford one.
And a 30-hour day's
out of the question, too, I suppose?
Okay, then.
How about just fewer headaches,
a small raise,
nighttime bladder control, and
a promise
that, fifty years from now
when I'm old and gray,
my child will remember all this
and call me blessed.

CALGON, TAKE ME AWAY

Okay, God, here I am for the
sixty-fifth time this week,
wiping pureed carrots off the wall.
Tonight, I have no doubt that
about the time I fall asleep,
harried and hopeful of a few hours' sleep,
she'll wake up howling and hungry.
And as sure as You'll send the sun up
tomorrow morning,
that mountain of soft and
spanking-clean diapers
will dwindle to none.
For this I gave up my glamorous,
well-paying, 40-hour-a-week job?

But for every spoonful of food
that gets slung, there's a smile
of sheer delight that follows.
For every hour of sleep I lose,
there's one gained for kisses and cuddles.
And for every diaper changed,
there's a dimpled darling waiting
to give as much love as I can take,
and to lift my weary spirit
one more time.
Thank You, Lord,
for helping it all balance out.

WHAT HAVE I GOTTEN MYSELF INTO?

Why did I do this, God?
I was supposed to be
a "woman of independence,"
and here I am instead
holding a miserably cranky,
monsoon-status wet,
very un-independent baby
on my hip.
Years of Chaucer and Shakespeare and Keats
echo now in my brain to songs sung by
Captain Kangaroo and Mr. Rogers and Big Bird.
Money that might have gone to Bloomingdale's
now goes to Beechnut, even faster.

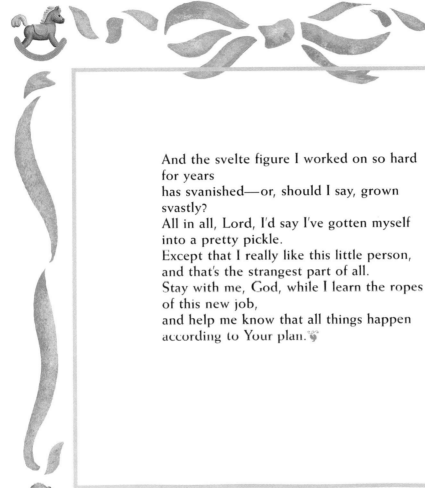

And the svelte figure I worked on so hard
for years
has svanished—or, should I say, grown
svastly?
All in all, Lord, I'd say I've gotten myself
into a pretty pickle.
Except that I really like this little person,
and that's the strangest part of all.
Stay with me, God, while I learn the ropes
of this new job,
and help me know that all things happen
according to Your plan.

Thoughts for Moments of Fascination

*There is a tomorrow coming by and by
when the lisper of the ABC will be the
master of a home of his own....*
Cuyler

NATURE'S WAY

"That's okay, Mommy, I know
you have to finish your work today.
I understand."
This pronouncement, Lord,
from a child who, a year ago,
barely talked?
The longer I'm a mother,
the more amazed I am at
the miracle of man.
What an awesome creature You created, Lord!
From crawling and walking to racing
upstairs…
from gurgling and giggling to "It's not nice
to say 'stupid,' is it, Mommy?"

I'm so grateful You picked me
to be Your partner in harvesting this life.
With reverence, I watch
as Your laws of nature develop his body.
With respect, I watch
as his yearning for learning
develops his mind.
With relief, I watch
as my obsession with social graces
develops his manners.
You weave it all together
so magnificently, Lord.
Help me to not let these hallowed threads
of today's child/tomorrow's promise
unravel.

And a Little Child Shall Lead Them

God, I watch in wonder
as this ringlet-crowned master of mayhem
crouches meekly beside
what used to be an earthworm
and remarks,
"How nice of these ants to come
visit this poor fellow!"
I marvel at his insightful grasp
of a dear friend's death:
"But, Mommy, that means
we won't see her anymore!"
How can it be, Father, that
a spirit so naive and so unsullied
spills forth such compassion
and wisdom and woe?

Father, are they Your eyes
that look so tenderly
on a fallen sparrow?
Are they Your hands reaching out
to comfort a teary-eyed toddler friend?
His time on earth has been so short, Lord,
yet, sometimes,
it seems he possesses the perceptions
of years.
God, help me guard that heart's pure love.
Help me shelter that sanguine soul
as long as possible.
And, please,
when childish dreams finally succumb
to grown-up doubts,
leave a little blind faith behind.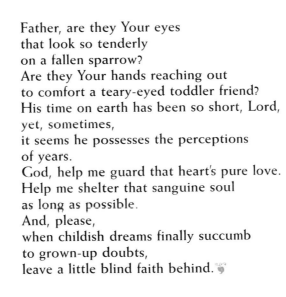

TO LOVE IS TO LEAD

Sitting here, watching my child
sleeping, Lord,
I'm struck by how perfect,
how contented, she is.
Those lashes long and feather-soft
against pink and porcelain velvet skin,
those deep, easy breaths
so completely devoid of any
sadness or stress or sin.
Lead me, Lord, as I introduce
this precious person
to the many phases and facets
of life on earth.
Help me make the pleasures richer.
Help me cradle the conflicts with love.
And always, Lord, help me lead her
back to You for
divine direction.

COMRADES

*I*t's a special time
for just the two of us, Lord.
Private victories
the world need never know.
Together,
we bask in our self-satisfaction,
in the smug rapture
spawned from fruition
of a significant event.
Thus, here we are—
with burgers and fries,
rented movies,
playground sand in our shoes,
a stack of library books,
two king-size bags of M&Ms,
and a list of other sybaritic delights
in which we plan to indulge ourselves.
Today we are enjoying life to its fullest,
honoring its richness,
commemorating several of its finest hours.
It's a mother-child moment
to remember forever
in our cherished mental scrapbook of life.

Thoughts for Moments of Trepidation

Thus hand in hand through life we'll go;
Its checkered paths of joy and woe
With cautious steps we'll tread.
Nathaniel Cotton

FIRST FAREWELL

Every expert I've read
says "it's crucial to get away"
and so I'm doing it.
But I have to tell You, God,
I'm not convinced.
Heaven knows I need a break—
and it's true I've certainly earned one,
but leave this little bundle of helplessness
behind?
Even the capable hands I've chosen
to care for her
can't possibly soothe her sobs as I could,
know her needs as I would.
And yet, I know this time must come,
if not now, then later.
Since it's now, I'm asking You, Lord,
to make this parting of our ways
less painful.
Make me mindful of the
significance of separations,
the value of vacations,
and the fact that it will always be over
all too soon.

BATTLE FATIGUE

God, I had to punish my child today,
for a whole morning of awful offenses.
He pulled the dog's tail.
He pushed the child next door.
He poured cereal all over the floor.
And he punched his cousin.
And when I tried to explain about
good manners and good citizenship
and a loving spirit,
he punched me, too.
So I took away Farmer Rabbit
and made him sit on his bed for ten minutes.
Then I explained again about good manners
and good citizenship and a loving spirit.
This time, he just looked at me
with huge, sad, wet gray eyes
and a chin that couldn't quite stay
in one place.
He'll be a better person someday,
but meanwhile,
we're both feeling rotten.
Help me remember, Lord, that
the guidance part of motherhood
is as critical as the love.

FEARFUL REFLECTIONS

S ometimes, Lord, I'm suddenly struck
   by the enormity of it all,
the breathtaking responsibility for
carrying this cherished child
from cradle to coffin.
Can I really do it, Lord?
Or was this something
You hadn't scheduled in Your
Master Plan?
I thought I was ready for motherhood,
for diapers and drooling
and stretch marks and skate boards
and colic and cliques and college funds.
But there's so much more to it than that.

There's sharing and trust
and love and forgiveness and losing,
winning and giving
and trying and failing and justice.
Who teaches me how to teach
those things, Lord?
Will she learn them at nursery school?
Do I sprinkle on little lectures
along with the baby powder?
I know I got me into this, God,
but please, won't You help me
get through it?

Hazard Duty

God, it's been one of those days.
Actually, it started last night
at 2 A.M....
continued at 3 A.M....
and again at 4.
Thus when daylight arrived at 6,
I wasn't especially elated to see it.
The baby was still crying,
my husband had no clean shirts,
there were dishes to be washed,
six thank-you notes to write,
my mother-in-law dropped by for a visit,
the dog threw up on the carpet,
the water was off for an hour,
I dropped a new quart of mayonnaise
on the floor,
and mangled a spoon in the garbage disposal.
Meanwhile, the baby is still crying.
Please, God,
help me remember You're always there,
and that tomorrow has tremendous potential
to be a better day.

COUNTDOWN

It's twenty minutes till eight, God.
Twenty minutes till my baby's not mine
anymore.
Now there'll be another
to perform the duties of mother.
While I'm writing out reports,
she'll be writing out ABCs.
While I'm setting up corporate meetings,
she'll be setting up building blocks.
While I'm gathering information,
she'll be gathering my little boy into her lap
for another round of "Pinocchio."
Is this the first crack in the bedrock, Lord?
The first blight on that bond
that began in the womb?
I don't know if this pain is worth the price
of a bigger house or better car, after all.
I'm not even sure my self-worth is worth this hurt.
What if the experts turn out to be wrong?
What if "quality time" just isn't time enough?
What if it's never, ever, the same again?
Please, God, get me out the door this first day,
past his outstretched arms and upturned eyes,
before I cry.

Thoughts for Moments of Reflection

*...a young child, a fresh, uncluttered mind,
a world before him—to what treasures will you lead him?
With what will you furnish his spirit?*
Gladys Hunt

Projections

I look at his eager face, Father,
  eyes sparkling,
lips spread in a smile that stretches
from one spaghetti-streaked cheek
to the other,
and I wonder what moments
life holds for him.
Will he be a Harvard boy, as Daddy hopes,
or a brilliant playwright (as Mom
secretly wishes)?
Will he marry? Father children?
Be wealthy? Famous? Friendly? Kind?
So much lies ahead,
so many crossroads and currents
and conflicts.

Please keep a watchful eye
on my little one, Lord.
Help me find the right paths
down which to send him,
say the right words to inspire him,
give the right advice to direct him.
Because whether he's a poet or a plumber
or a president or a priest,
he'll still need to be loved
by us both.

DAY OF DISCOVERY

The serious stuff is behind us, God—
whether to buy a Mickey Mouse or
Donald Duck lunch box...
red or blue Converse hightops...
two days a week or three.
Now we're left only with
opening Miss Tricia's door
on this first day of nursery school.
With best clothes on, best smile on,
and admonitions for best behavior,
he takes an excited but unsure step toward
the world of the future.

Big Bird is almost behind him now;
in his place, a tiny kitchen
with removable sink and plastic pork chops,
the Pledge of Allegiance,
red tempera paint apples,
and nineteen new faces to bemuse and befriend.
Lord, please wrap Your loving arms around him
as he makes his way into their midst.
Open his eyes to the joys of learning,
the self-satisfaction of trying,
the exultation of success.
And, Lord, endow Miss Tricia with
unlimited love.

GROWING PAINS

Just yesterday, God,
she was a tiny thing,
squirming, helpless and loud,
in her eyelet-trimmed,
oak-barred boudoir.
Now look at her:
like some caricatured Amazon goddess,
she flings about dolls and balls
and books,
then cheers in wild abandon
upon reviewing the melee.
I, too, cheer for her grand achievements,
yet there's a part of me, Lord,
that succumbs to
a tear or two.

For every jubilant step she takes alone,
every puzzle piece she guides swiftly
into place,
snips another thread
in the mother/child towrope.
God, I know it's a rope that is meant
to be severed,
replaced by anchors holding each of us
strong and steady,
but it still hurts a little
every time I see her grow.
Can You help it not to?

My Do It

How quickly, Father,
he's moved from mashed bananas
to mashed fingers.
Those chubby legs once flawless
and laced in white kid
now give testament to the
agony and ecstasy of mobile independence.
"My do it!" comes the indignant cry as,
day after day,
one by one,
tasks move from my domain to his.
Lord, help me not to wince too hard
when I know the fall is coming.
Help me hold my tongue
when the word is on the tip
of his.
Most of all, Father,
help me savor every moment
of these wonderful days of discovery,
rejoicing in his exuberance and
reveling in my own.

LOVE SONG

"Mommy, I missed you!"
What a way to end my day!
Thank You, God, for choosing me
to be the mother of this child.
This child who, as an infant,
rarely cried.
This child who, even at two,
was tolerable.
This child who now hangs suspended
from my neck, doggie shoes
and grandmother crafted jammies
adding that much more allure
to apple-sticky lips and immovable arms.
"I missed you, too!" I tell him.
Lord, let him know how much!
Let him know how his hugs restore me,
how his jubilant kisses renew me,
how his stories and songs inspire me,
how his daily achievements uplift me.
If I died tomorrow, Father,
resolutely I would go
for having known the rejuvenating joy
of this little child's love.

Thoughts for Moments of Frustration

ù

Finish every day and be done with it.
You have done what you could.
Ralph Waldo Emerson

SECOND THOUGHTS

G od, I don't want to be a mother today.
I don't even want to be a wife!
What happened to my time?
What's happened to my life?
The gang on the Third Floor of Edna Moore
would never believe that I,
voted by them in college as
"The girl least likely to be domesticated,"
am now so deplorably domestic
I can't find time to shave my legs.
Worthwhile causes?
Come on, God, who's got time for causes,
worthy or not,
when there's a baby in the house?

Experienced mothers—those who have
children who've made it to age three—
tell me it gets easier.
But the veterans—those mothers
harboring teenagers at home—
tell me now is the time to enjoy.
I need a lightning bolt, Lord,
or a burning bush, or perhaps
a visit from good old Gabriel
as a sign I will have a life of my own
again.
Someday.
I hope.

No Win, No Way

W hat do I do now, Lord?
I got past the first day,
the first sitter,
the first deadline.
But now I face
the first choice.
Do I play Concerned Employee
or Caring Parent?
How in the world do I rank
a nursery school picnic
against a Skills Management Workshop?
I wish it was 1880, when
the toughest choice a mother ever faced
was whether to confront fierce Indians
or a crop-threatening famine.

Dead or alive,
at least she'd emerge a hero.
I don't even know what to pray for, God,
except a clone,
or a hurricane,
or an uncharacteristic wave
of tolerance and understanding in
my child and my boss.
Mostly, Lord,
I just need You to help me get through this,
and consider scheduling rain
for next Friday at eleven.

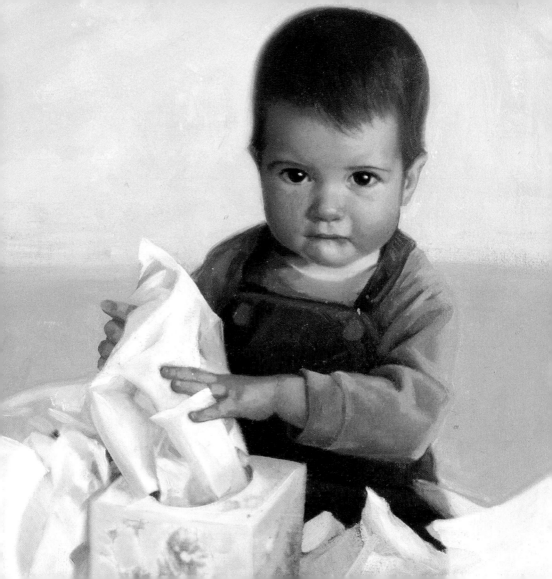

Thoughts for Moments of Desperation

*Lord, make me a channel of thy peace…
That where there is despair I may bring hope.*
St. Francis of Assisi

GRANDDAD IS GONE

Dear God, I hurt so badly.
I've lost my daddy,
the man who tossed me into the air,
rode me in his Jeep, chased away the ghosts,
tucked me into bed,
did everything Mama did—just a little bit bigger.
But if he was a hero to me at 30,
what superhuman persona must he have been
to my little child?
Granddad's been there every day
of her short, simple life,
for bear hugs and butterfly hunts
and two cookies every time Mommy said, "Only one."
How do I tell her, Lord?
How does a little one understand about death?
Will she think I'll leave her next?
Will she fear sharing love anymore?
Please help me ease her confusion.
Help her know that while Granddad's body is gone,
his spirit will last forever,
hers to cherish and learn from for life.
And, God, most importantly,
help us know that he lives on in us.

WHEN LOVE HURTS

Help me, God.
My child is sick.
That precious face is listless now,
forehead hot and eyelids heavy.
That sweet, sinless spirit,
restrained and restless.
It seems so wrong
for a child to hurt,
and I feel so helpless.
Please, God, let him know
how much I love him,
how much I hurt when he does.
Use my hands to heal him.
Use my heart to reach out to him.
Use my head to stay strong
and calm and resourceful.
And, Father, if it be Your will,
I ask You, please, to
make my child happy and whole and healthy
before the morrow.

IMPRUDENT ESTRANGEMENT

God, my worst nightmare came to life today.
I looked up and my child wasn't there.
Wasn't standing next to the mannequin
she always finds so intriguing,
wasn't crawling around under the blouse racks
she usually finds so appealing,
wasn't making faces at herself in the mirror,
where I left her, two feet away.
My heart was leaden ice
and a voice in my head echoed,
"You irresponsible fool!," as
I frantically hunted and called
and cried.
Thirty-five minutes later,
somebody found her,
asleep in a cardboard carton
in the corner of a storage room.

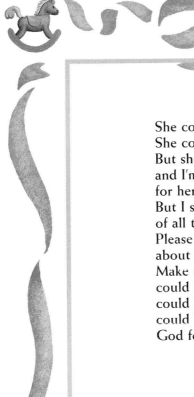

She could have been anywhere.
She could have not been there at all.
But she was, and she was safe,
and I'm so grateful to You, Lord,
for her protection.
But I still need You in the aftermath
of all this.
Please make me not feel so guilty
about turning my back.
Make me know it has happened to others,
could happen to anyone,
could happen again,
could have been worse...
God forbid. 🌑

Thoughts for Moments of Celebration

A year old yesterday! You winsome thing,
Blithe as a nestling twittering in the spring!
Victor Hugo

ONE TO GROW ON

Lord, here's another birthday—
she's growing up so fast!
Diapers, teething crackers, and pull toys
seem years behind us now as she
skips around in her lavender tights,
icing from her personally selected
Care Bears chocolate cake smeared from
eyebrow to elbow to knee.
Ah, this is a happy day, Father—
a day for giggles and games
and giving.
Giving gifts, like the ballerina music box
I want her to have until she's a hundred…

giving love (or ladylike tolerance, at least) to
six small friends who've shared everything
from first colds to first trikes and, who,
hopefully,
will share cake and secrets
for years to come...
giving memories, to all of us, of
a crisp, clean, sunshiny day
when all was right in our world,
there were two helpings of everything
for everyone,
nobody cried, nobody threw up,
nobody's feelings got hurt, and
even the dog was sorry to see the afternoon end.
Thank You, God, for days of
divine intervention.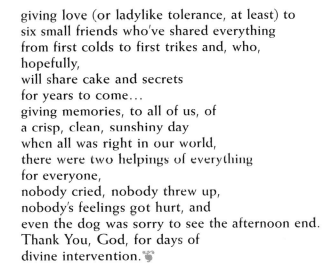

TRIBUTE TO LIFE

*I*t's a day for trumpets and truffles, Lord—
a day for cameras and canapés!
My little one's home from the hospital,
all signs of that damnable disease
expelled from her body forever.
It's a day to rejoice and revel, Lord—
a day to thank You for Your infinite kindness
and guidance and strength.
See how willingly my angel shares
her timid, crooked smile?
How delightedly she giggles forth
to claim Aunt Carolyn's hug?

I do believe in miracles, God—
in the love of friends and
support of strangers
and prayers of both.
My prayer to You, Father,
of this golden-haired gift of gleefulness
snatched from the heinous hands of Death,
is a simple one:
Lead us beyond this valley
of the shadow of sadness;
heal our weary bodies, minds, and souls;
and help us to never forget the joy
of each new morning's first virgin breath.

THE BEST JOB IN THE WORLD

This job's a tough one, Lord,
but the perks are beyond compare.
Who else but a mother
knows the joy of satisfying
a human being's every need?
Who else but a mother
sees love come alive a hundred ways,
from jelly-smeared kisses and
diminishing sobs
to crayoned Valentines
and soggy, shared suckers?
God, thank You so much for this
priceless privilege,
this role so few ever know.
Inadequate as my training,
inept as I might be,
I know I have tenure for life.
Even so, I ask Your assistance
in making sure I deserve it.
For a bad mother is the worst nightmare
a child can ever know,
and a good one, a dream come true
to curl up with for life.